You Can't Park an Elephant in a Car Park

Written by Judith Nicholls
Illustrated by Tim Archbold

Collins *Educational*
An imprint of HarperCollins*Publishers*

Andrew Slater came to school…

on an elephant called Lord Fred.
His teacher fell down in a faint,
and from the floor she said...

"You can't bring an *elephant* to school,
it simply can't be done.
An *elephant* does his sums in a *zoo*.
So please, move on!"

"But Fred can share my lunch," said Andrew, "then join in PE!"
"You can check with Mrs Banner, but I'm *sure* she won't agree."

"I can't have an *elephant* doing PE,
it simply can't be done.
He's got no pumps or T-shirt.
Now please, move on!"

So Andrew left for the shoe shop,
to see what he could find.

The man turned pale and whispered,
"I don't want to be unkind, but…

you can't buy *shoes* for an *elephant*,
it simply can't be done.
Everyone knows there's no space
for his toes.
So please, move on!"

The sports shop girl looked jolly,
and her T-shirts looked quite wide.
"I'd like one for my friend, please."
She laughed until she cried!

"You can't buy *him* a T-shirt,
it simply can't be done.
Hasn't he got one in his *trunk*?
Now please, move on!"

Poor Andrew rode on down the town and to the grocer's shop.
He'd just climbed off when PC Harris frowned and called out "STOP!"

"You can't park *him* in the car park,
it simply can't be done.
An *elephant* parks in an *elephant park*.
So please, move on!"

The day was hot and Andrew thought,
"What fun to be missing school.
Now why not take Fred for a nice cool swim,
in the local swimming pool?"

"I can't give *him* a ticket,
it simply can't be done.
No one swims without their trunks.
Now please, move on!"

"But he's *got* his *trunk*!" cried Andrew, and his face spread into a grin. "Oh, *please* miss, give him a ticket and let us in."

"Well… I can't say *no* to an *elephant*,
it simply can't be done.
So in you go, and mind my toe,
and put his *armbands* on!"

The lifeguard blinked as Fred dived in, and the children yelled for a ride.

They coaxed him up the diving board, they nudged him down the slide.

They taught him breaststroke,

backstroke,

crawl.

They taught him butterfly.

And Andrew Slater smiled again as he sang with a happy sigh…

"You *can* take an elephant swimming, it really *can* be done…

but, just make sure he wears his *trunk* and puts his *armbands* on!"